Soccer Refereeing - Whistling For Fun

by Barry Corrall

Cartoons by Wendy

EDITOR
Michael Robinson

Price
£4.95

British Library Cataloguing in Publication Data
A catalogue record for this book is available from the British Library
ISBN 0-947808-63-9

Copyright © 1995; SOCCER BOOK PUBLISHING LTD.
72, St. Peters' Avenue, Cleethorpes,
Sth. Humberside, DN35 8HU, England   Tel. (01472-696226)

All rights are reserved. No part of this publication may be reproduced, stored into a retrieval system or transmitted, in any form or by any means, electronic, mechanical, photocopying, recording, or otherwise, without the prior written permission of Soccer Book Publishing Ltd.

**Printed by Adlard Print & Typesetting Services, The Old School, Village Green, Ruddington, Notts.
Typset by Marksman Publications (01472) 601893**

CONTENTS

Foreword 5

Chapter 1 - Shattered Dreams 7

Chapter 2 - Become A Referee 9

Chapter 3 - Benefits And Rewards 11

Chapter 4 - Making A Start 19

Chapter 5 - Necessary Equipment 23

Chapter 6 - Personal Presentation 25

Chapter 7 - Communication With Players - And Others 29

Chapter 8 - Use Your Experience & Avoid Being Too Clever! 33

Chapter 9 - Take Responsibility 37

Chapter 10 - Watch Play At All Times 39

Chapter 11 - The 'Pyramid' System 42

Chapter 12 - Jack Swain - the first of the few 47

Chapter 13 - Personal Recollections 49

Chapter 14 - Refereeing Nightmares 58

Strange Refereeing Occurrences 64

FOREWORD

When Barry Corrall approached Soccer Book Publishing Ltd. with his ideas for a book about Soccer Refereeing, he did not need to tell me that there has never been such a book available. As an ex-referee myself, I well remember the difficulties which I encountered in 1969 when I decided to hang up my boots and reach for a whistle!

I was fortunate because I had a referee friend who steered me in the right direction, but I was only too well aware of the difficulties prospective referees face.

However, we felt that we should go beyond a simple summary of 'how to become a referee' - by revealing some of the drawbacks as well as the advantages of the past-time.

We think that Barry's humorous, chatty style brings much of the text to life and have thrown in a few oddities and amusing incidents to round-off the book.

John Robinson

Publisher

CHAPTER 1

Shattered Dreams

Was your greatest dream to be another Paul Gascoigne?

Perhaps you saw yourself at Wembley, turning on the magic footwork and helping England towards a World-Cup victory.

There you were, dribbling your way into the opposition penalty-area, leaving a trail of well beaten defenders behind you. Now there was only the goalkeeper between you and glory. Sixty-thousand England fans go suddenly quiet, their breaths held as you come to a halt in front of goal.

You stand there with your foot on the ball, inviting the 'keeper to come and take it from you. He accepts the challenge and rushes towards you.

As he gets near, you casually flick the ball up on to your thigh, and from there into the air. The 'keeper is almost upon you now; but just as it seems he may claim the ball, you rise with a majestic leap and head it over his flailing arms. The ball loops tantalizingly through the air, and after one bounce nestles cosily in the back of the net.

The crowd are cheering, and chanting your name. Gary Lineker is patting you on the back in congratulation: even the stricken goalkeeper stands there in admiration of your skill and applauds you.

The referee blows his whistle for the end of the game: you have scored the winning goal in the last minute of the World Cup Final.

Perhaps something like this, was your dream, and nothing was going to stop you from fulfilling it.

But then you discovered something about yourself. For some strange reason, you had been given legs that would refuse to act the way you wanted them to. No matter how you tried, whenever you attempted to kick a ball, you either missed it completely or tripped over that undisciplined, non-kicking leg.

You found that the only dribbling you ever managed successfully was, on visiting the dentist, when trying to swill your mouth out through frozen lips.

Perhaps your footballing efforts have at times been subjected to ridicule by others more fortunately blessed in the leg-department? Well, so what? Don't be downhearted: be positive - take a refereeing course and become a referee.

CHAPTER 2

Become A Referee

Even if you are not totally without footballing skills, and are a useful player, becoming a referee would give you another string to your bow. It is possible to carry on playing and, at the same time, learn the trade of refereeing.

Personally, if I were fourteen again and as aware as I am now of what can be achieved, I would begin immediately to make determined efforts to get right to the top of refereeing.

Unfortunately for me, my sole interest in football had always been in playing or watching it. I had never given a thought to refereeing.

My playing days finished at the age of thirty-seven: I missed the involvement in football so much, that three years later I took the advice of a referee friend of mine, and enrolled on a refereeing course.

Of course, starting at the age of forty has restricted me as far as promotion is concerned. I cannot emphasise enough, that it really is an advantage to start while you are young, if you wish to climb to the top.

And by the way, let me just mention here that this part of the book is not intended for males alone. There is a place for females in refereeing, and there are a number of them doing very well at this moment. Indeed, there is a whisper in official circles that in the not too distant future, females will be refereeing in the top grade of soccer in the UK. Who knows? - perhaps one day there may even be a thriving Ladies Professional Football League here as in Italy.

Soccer Refereeing - Whistling for Fun

So, come on ladies, don't be shy. The only qualification you need is to have reached fourteen years of age. Therefore, boys and girls, men and women, why not take my advice and go for it yourselves? Believe me, the rewards can be great.

CHAPTER 3

Benefits And Rewards

With the well organized youth football that exists today, young people are being encouraged more and more to try refereeing. And after all, what's wrong with wanting to become another Philip Don or Mike Reed, two of the finest refs around at this moment in time?

Imagine what it would be like to become a referee and progress through the ranks, to eventually take charge of an F.A. or World Cup Final. Starting at such a young age presents that possibility to the youth of today.

There are many benefits to be gained from refereeing even if you have no ambition to get to the very top of the pile, but would be content to officiate solely in junior football: plenty of fresh air and exercise - opportunities to meet new people and perhaps make new friends.

Your local Referee's Association (R.A.) will welcome you into their fold. There you can talk to other refs and gain all sorts of useful information. You will always find someone there willing to help with any problems or queries you might have. The latest changes to the 'Laws Of The Game' are discussed; other referees' problems, and many other talking points are aired. Very often, well-known personalities are invited to the monthly meetings to give a talk, and answer questions. Managers, players, coaches and sometimes top class referees are invited guests at R.A. meetings... Most R.A.'s hold functions such as dinners, dances and other social get-togethers. So, as well as keeping you healthy and fit, refereeing can provide you with an active social life too.

If you wish to progress to the higher echelons of 'reffing' and are successful in so doing, the rewards become greater...

Travel

If you progress up the refereeing ladder and reach the semi-professional level of football, you would be required to visit various towns and cities in Great Britain. Then, should you progress to the top of the ladder, other countries, and even continents, could be your destination.

Recognition

At this point, let me introduce to you a referee acquaintance of mine - Alan Seville. Alan was an official on the Football League from 1974 to 1991. He was reputed to be the smallest 'man in black' in the business. But, though small in stature, Alan was one of the fittest and, in my opinion, one of the best referees around in this period of his career.

During the course of his years in League Football, Alan has blown his whistle on most of the famed grounds throughout England... Highbury, Anfield, Old Trafford, White Hart Lane and many others. At the time this book is being written, he is serving football as an Assessor.

Every referee on the Football League is continually being assessed by someone like Alan. This means that they are being monitored to ensure that a good standard is maintained.

Alan says it always surprises him that he is often recognised at football grounds, even now. Fans will engage him in conversation about matches which he has refereed. A lot of these people now number amongst his friends.

When I asked Alan what he had gained most from his career in refereeing, his immediate reply was: "Certainly not pots of money." (Perhaps he was unfortunate in this respect. Payments to referees in the world of pro-football have increased quite substantially in recent times. An Endsleigh

Benefits And Rewards

League referee now receives in excess of £150 per game. Linesmen collect approximately 50% of that figure. A Premiership ref' earns substantially more).

Alan says he has drawn more pleasure from meeting people, than from any other facet of the game: "People who I had never dreamed of meeting. People who I had read about, talked about and looked up to in the game of soccer." He spoke of Nat Lofthouse, Tom Finney, Stan Cullis, Jimmy Greaves, Bobby Charlton and many others.

Some of these names may be unfamiliar to you, but most of the older generation will tell you that these names are of giant personalities in the

Alan Seville, Football League referee, warning a player.

Soccer Refereeing - Whistling for Fun

Another job of League referees and linesmen is to be photographed with the opposing team captains and mascots

game of football.

And yet some of these, and other famous people, have demonstrated great respect towards Alan as a referee. Let me provide an example: Alan was due to referee a game involving Nottingham Forest. There had been a bad motorway accident which meant many fans would possibly arrive late at the ground. Alan was sitting in his dressing-room giving match instructions to his linesmen, when in walked Brian Clough (then Forest's manager). "Excuse me, sir. Are we going to kick off on time tonight?" he asked.

Alan replied, "As soon as I know, Mr. Clough, you will know. With police advice I will make a decision nearer to kick off time". Whereupon Brian Clough smiled and said, "Thank you sir, that is good enough for me."

Like me, Alan has long been an admirer of Cloughie, so to be shown such genuine respect by the man meant a lot to him.

Confidence and Self-Belief

These are the benefits I have gained most from my own refereeing exploits.

I think gaining confidence in refereeing has to be a gradual process. I have found my own developed as a result of having to deal with players and situations which have arisen.

I, myself, experienced a great boost to my confidence very early in my refereeing career. In fact, it was in only the third match I had been charged with since successfully completing the referee's course…

The game was about ten minutes into the second half. I was quietly congratulating myself on how smoothly things seemed to be going.

The team playing in stripes were launching an attack. The ball was played up to the centre-forward. As he shaped to control it, the ball hit a lump of mud and bounced up. The centre-forward instinctively knocked it down with his hand; a clear case of deliberate handball. I blew my whistle to indicate the offence. The centre-forward then made it plainly obvious he disagreed with my decision: "You must be ******* joking. Don't be such a ****", he said, from somewhere up in the clouds. Yes, you've guessed it; he was about six feet-fourteen, and had muscles on his fingernails. (Here I will quote one of the parts of Law Twelve: 'If in the opinion of the referee a player is guilty of using foul or abusive language, he shall be sent from the field of play').

Soccer Refereeing - Whistling for Fun

So you see the situation; obviously this giant had to go. I hadn't had occasion to even caution anyone in my first two games. Now I thought I might be facing the possible prospect of getting my nose punched by a colossus on football studs.

I walked across to where he was standing, glaring at me, taking my little notebook out as I did so. I braced myself in readiness for the ordeal. "Okay, player, let's have the name", I said, with as much coolness as I could muster. My pencil then dropped from my trembling hand to the ground. Hoping this had gone unnoticed and not wanting to show any signs of weakness, I merely trod it into the mud, then produced a spare one from my pocket.

"But ref, I wasn't talking to you, honest", he said, his granite-like face a picture of hurt innocence.

"Look, I wasn't born yesterday. Just give me your name please", I said pitilessly. While I spoke, I was attempting to look as casual as I could, as if: "I've send hundreds of blokes off before mate, and all of 'em have been twice as big as you".

I informed him that I was sending him off for using foul language. I then waited for his mallet-like fist to crash down on top of my head, driving me into the mud.

I was overjoyed and relieved when he simply turned on his heel and walked slowly off the pitch. Of course he was muttering a few niceties to himself on the way, but what the heck - I had survived.

But there was one more unnerving moment to come. After I had blown the final whistle, I saw him approaching me; this time he was dressed in his 'civvies'. This was going to be the pay-off I thought, preparing my forty-year old legs for flight.

He looked down on me from the heights. "Sorry about that ref, but I really wasn't talking to you. I was shouting at our manager on the touchline, 'cause he was waving his flag."

I looked him in the eye - albeit at a forty-five degree angle. Then with more bravado than was good for me I said, "As I say son, I wasn't born yesterday. I was born the day before."

He actually laughed at my weak effort of a joke, then held out his hand for me to shake. "Well done anyway ref. You had an excellent game." With that he walked off, leaving me standing there testing my knuckles for broken bones, and intending to grant my guardian angel an extended contract.

Looking back, I think this episode instilled a great deal of confidence into me. I was relieved but very pleased with myself, for having come through my first refereeing confrontation so well. There were many others in the years that followed, but this first one was, I think, the ultimate test and confidence builder.

CHAPTER 4

Making A Start

If at this point, what you have read has whet your appetite, and you have made up your mind you would like to have a shot at refereeing, here is how to go about it.

Before embarking on a referee's coaching course, however, my advice is to buy yourself a **Referee's Chart**. This is the working manual for all whistle-blowers. It contains not only the seventeen **Laws Of The Game**, but also a certain amount of advice to referees.

If you know a referee personally, I would suggest that you ask him/her to read it through with you. The referee could then explain areas of the laws, which perhaps you may not be clear about. This would, I feel, help you and give you a good start on your course.

Persuading a friend to accompany you on the course is a good idea. After each session you could test each other on what you have been taught. I guarantee this would help you both to absorb the knowledge more fully.

Where Courses are Held

This is the first piece of information you require, and there are a number of ways of obtaining this:

(i) Local **Sports Papers** run advertisements giving dates and venues, but first of all contact your local Referee's Association (see below for further information).

(ii) There is almost certain to be someone attached to your **Local Football Club** who may be able to help and the 'Football in the Community

Soccer Refereeing - Whistling for Fun

Schemes' run by the Professional Clubs are a valuable source of information.

(iii) A **School Sports Teacher** could well have the necessary knowledge but, almost certainly, the best source of this type of information will be your local **County Football Association**.

Look in the telephone directory under the heading of whatever town you live in. For instance, if you live in Birmingham, look for - Birmingham County Football Association. Then either ring or write to the secretary of that association, asking for the name and address - or telephone number - of the secretary of your local **Referee's Association**.

That person will advise you of where and when the next courses will be taking place: you will also be told how the course is constructed. Usually they are over a period of six to eight weeks - one night a week - two hours per night.

Once on the course, you need to listen carefully to your coach - study the laws very thoroughly - and above all take what you are doing seriously. The more you put into the course, the more you will get out of it; a thorough understanding of the laws will stand you in good stead as a referee.

At this point I will assume you have taken the course and completed it successfully. The next step for you is to again contact your local County F.A., to apply for official registration as a referee.

If you are between the ages of fourteen and sixteen years old, you will apply for registration as a **Youth Class** referee. If you have reached the age of sixteen, you will apply as a **Class Three** referee.

The application form you are required to fill in, will tell you how much you need to pay for whichever class you are applying for.

Making A Start

After a short time, you will receive your registration card, together with a receipt for the registration fee you have paid.

At this stage you are an officially registered referee. What you need to do now is find yourself a league in which to operate.

If you are a Youth Class referee, I would advise you to pick a League which caters for the lower age groups: the Under 10 age group is the ideal player age for a young referee to begin his/her career in refereeing.

If you are sixteen and have qualified as a Class Three, you are in fact entitled to take charge in **Open Age** soccer matches. Personally under the age of 20 I do not think this is such a good idea. I believe in the old adage - 'you must learn to walk before you can run.' For my money, Youth Leagues are the ideal environment in which to begin learning the refereeing trade.

When you are accepted by a league, you could make it clear to the league secretary that you wish to operate initally in the lower age groups, perhaps until the time arrives when you feel confident enough to handle the older players. I would suggest under 13's as your top age limit until such confidence is acquired.

Between under 10 and under 13 there is little in the way of 'hassle' from the players; though to be truthful, their parents can be a problem. (I will let you know my thoughts on this, and offer some advice later in the book).

Older Class Three referees should apply to their respective local adult leagues and do not, of course, need to deal with the 'lower-age' leagues.

CHAPTER 5

Necessary Equipment

Here is a list of basic equipment for your kit-bag:

SHIRT - (Black)

SHORTS - (Black)

SOCKS - (Black with White tops)

BOOTS - (Black - No fancy colours)

FLAGS - (One Red, One Yellow)

WHISTLE - (At least two)

PENCIL - (At least two)

WATCH - (Two if possible)

COIN - (To toss-up with)

TIE-UPS - (Two - to hold socks up)

NOTEBOOK - (For cautions and other notes if necessary!)

It is a good idea to keep a list such as this in your kit-bag. Then before you start out for the game you are going to referee, you can check each item as you put it in your bag.

Take it from me, it is so easy to forget something vital!

I remember on one occasion when I was due to referee an inter-garage game, in the West-Midland Passenger Transport League. After changing into my ref's outfit, I began sorting out my equipment. I found flags, notebook, pencils, coin and stopwatch; but my legs turned to jelly when I realised there was a deficiency in the whistle department: it turned out that my two-year-old, magpie-type son had raided my bag, and pilfered them out of their box. The crafty little devil had even replaced the lid tightly, so I would not notice they were missing.

When I told the W.M.P.T. storeman about my predicament, he turned his stores upside-down trying to find a substitute whistle. I was waiting impatiently outside, when I heard him give out a cry of triumph. Yes, he had found a whistle; it was an ancient bus-inspector's whistle. I thought - 'at least I'm not going to have to whistle with my fingers.'

But the snag was, the sound that issued from this whistle, was an octave higher than that from a normal one.

I demonstrated it to the players before the kick-off, with the hope they would recognize the sound during the game. But each time I blew the whistle in the early part of the match, players would look at me and laugh. And when I tried to blow the thing hard, it was worse, because the pea just got jammed and the sound that came out was pathetically weak. So remember, it never hurts to check and double check. It can save you a lot of embarrassment.

CHAPTER 6

Personal Presentation

At the time of writing, I have been manager of a local boys team, since they were Under 10, to their present age of Under 16. So it is with my manager's hat on now that I speak, when I emphasise the need for referees of all ages to present themselves well.

Whenever you referee an official game, someone (usually the manager) from both teams will award you marks out of ten. As well as being based on performance, appearance and personality are important factors also. This means that even before you blow the whistle to start a game, you can either gain or lose marks. So the way you conduct yourself is important.

At all times, be respectful to the people you have to deal with. On your arrival at a ground, always find the managers of both teams. When you have done this, introduce yourself in a polite and pleasant manner:

"Excuse me, are you the manager of ____?"

If the answer is 'yes', then tell them your name and inform them that you are their referee for the day.

Using an approach along these lines will create a good first impression. Put this together with a smart appearance - polished boots, shirt and shorts well-pressed, hair neat and tidy: now you will feel and look the part, and this will get you off on the right foot with the people you are in contact with. But I am a firm believer anyway that, if you yourself know you look good, you will perform better as a referee.

Soccer Refereeing - Whistling for Fun

Like myself, there are those who, as well as being a team manager, are qualified referees. If you are refereeing a game where there is such a person involved, never dismiss without consideration, any advice that person may offer you, no matter how trivial you consider it.

I well remember an instance which will serve to illustrate the significance of that statement:

My team were involved in a quarter-final of a Cup competition: we were in the dressing room prior to the match. I had just finished my pre-match talk, and there were some fifteen minutes to kick-off time.

I decided to check whether the referee had arrived, as he had not made his presence known. I opened the door of the referee's dressing-room and stepped inside.

I might have thought I had walked into a steamy turkish-bath, if it had not been for the pungent smell of cigarettes.

I flapped my hands about in an effort to penetrate the nicotine curtain, and find its source. Slowly the murk cleared, and there in the far corner, was the scruffiest, most seedy-looking excuse for a referee I have ever clapped eyes on.

'Are you our ref?" I asked, between coughs: (I hoped - no, prayed - his answer might be perhaps - "No, I've come to unblock the drains." Or - "No, I'm a tramp and this is where I always doss down.").

Unfortunately for me though, the answer came back - Yeah, I am. Whereabouts is the 'bog', mate?"

When I had recovered from the shock, I directed him to the toilet and off he slouched: two minutes later he returned. I guessed his age to be around seventeen or eighteen; but though his face was youthful, his slovenly manner made him seem much older.

I felt I wanted to pick him up and shake him, with a view to livening him

Personal Presentation

up. Instead though, I offered him some advice.

I had noticed he had tied his bootlaces in such a way that the bows were flapping about when he walked. I pointed out to him that this is potentially dangerous: I once saw a player slide-tackle another player, whereupon the tackler's studs got caught up in the other player's lace bow. The result was a broken leg for each player.

Since that occurence I have always tucked my own laces in, out of harm's way, whether playing or refereeing. I have passed this on to players of my own team, and they saw the sense of it: but this individual mumbled something incoherently through the cigarette clamped in his lips, and so I left him to himself. When he made his appearance on to the pitch, I saw that he had chosen to ignore my words - as I expected he would.

His performance in the game was as deplorable as his appearance and personality. He failed to keep up with play, and spent most of his time in the centre-circle. The only time he broke into anything resembling a 'sprint', was when the ball was played into one or other of the penalty-areas.

It was just such an occasion, when our centre-forward broke clear of the opposing defence - the score was 0-0 with two minutes left to play. He had only the goalkeeper to beat: he knocked the ball to one side of the 'goalie', and was about to hit it into the net, when he was 'rugby tackled' by the 'keeper - a clear penalty; not even this referee could fail to judge it so; or so I thought.

But when hearing no whistle, I looked in the direction of the centre-circle, (guessing that might be where he would be found) and saw him sitting on the ground, disentangling the studs of one boot from the lace-bow of the other.

Consequently, he did not see the incident, and we were denied a penalty.

Soccer Refereeing - Whistling for Fun

The score stayed at 0-0 and extra-time was played. We lost 1-0 in extra-time, so went out of the Cup.

If only he had acted on the advice of someone far more experienced than himself, my team would have almost certainly gone into the semi-final. More importantly, from his point of view, he might have earned one more mark from myself. As it was, I could not bring myself to award him more than four out of ten.

When a manager awards four or less marks to a referee, he is obliged to send in a written report to the County F.A. This I did. I would imagine I might not be the last one to do so. Whether this is so or not I have no way of knowing, but I have not seen that referee again to this day.

CHAPTER 7

Communication With Players - And Others

When refereeing very young players, it is important for you to remember that they are very much at a learning stage. In your role as a referee, you can play an important part in their football education.

The taking of throw-ins for example: if a young player takes a throw-in incorrectly whilst I am refereeing, I will apply the law and whistle for a foul-throw. However, before allowing the other team to take the re-throw, I will hold play up briefly - I will then explain, and show by demonstration, what was wrong with the throw: then I will indicate, again by demonstration, the correct way.

My thinking is, that if youngsters are not corrected at an early stage, they might well develop bad habits.

Unfortunately, there have been odd occasions when parents/spectators, have voiced their objections to my methods: "Let them get on with it, ref' - it's only a throw-in. They're only kids and you're spoiling their game."

With all due respect to anyone who may feel this way - their thinking is misguided. From my experience of coaching young footballers, I have found they want to learn how to do things in the correct manner.

I am certain that far from lessening their enjoyment, this enhances it.

However, if you do enounter loud disagreement from the line for those

Soccer Refereeing - Whistling for Fun

reasons, do not be afraid to take action: hold play up for a little while longer: walk calmly in the direction of the source of complaints: stop a few yards short of it - then, rather than singling out any one individual, if there are more than one, speak to all in general. Explain that you are trying to prevent young players from developing bad habits, by showing them the correct methods.

Then you might say something along these lines:

"I'm doing my best to help them, and I would appreciate your help by allowing me to do that. Thank you."

It may seem a daunting task for you to take this sort of action, and to speak to adults in this fashion. But providing your manner is polite and respectful, I am confident that in most cases the respect will be returned.

Besides, it is always advisable to nip in the bud any sort of over-loud interference from spectators, rather than allow it to grow into something worse.

Thankfully, I can assure you that for the large majority of the time, I myself have received congratulations from football people, for refereeing in this manner.

Good communication with your linesmen is important. Always let them know what you expect from them. This applies at whatever level you are refereeing.

For now though, we will concentrate on club linesmen in youth football.

A club linesman is someone who will volunteer - one from each team - to run the line for you. In most instances he will be the manager, or a parent of one of the players.

Now, I am positive that these people always have the best intentions. But

Communication With Players - And Others

football is a game of passion; even if it is being played by nine-year olds.

It is always going to be difficult for someone to be completely unbiased, when attached in some way with a football team. So being given a flag by a referee who gives him no pre-match instructions, may well tempt him to want to run things the way he sees fit.

So when you meet your club linesmen, give them as little responsibillity as possible. My own pre-match instructions to them are usually along these lines: "Give me a flag for all offsides - I will decide if there is interference; signal for throw-ins, goal-kicks and corners, when the whole of the ball is over the line. If you do flag for offside and I want to carry on, I will hold my arm aloft to let you know I have seen you - please then lower your flag."

Then I will let them know whether I want them to operate on a left or right-wing diagonal.

Occasionally, a club linesman may ask if you require him to indicate any foul play. Because young players are limited on the distance they can kick a ball, it is reasonably easy to keep up with the action. So my answer to that question is always: "If I am not up with play and you think you see an offence, raise your flag. But if I am reasonably well placed to judge for myself, leave it to me."

I then make sure I am always within about fifteen yards of the action so, consequently, the linesman is not saddled with undue responsibility.

Furthermore, always try to cover as much ground as you can. Using the diagonal system, (which you should have had explained to you on the course) travel from goal-line to goal-line, and touch-line to touch-line.

If you are close to the action when making a decision, your judgement is more likely to be accepted by all. Being forty or fifty yards away when blowing for an infringement can leave the way open for dissent - even when you are spot on.

Give nice, crisp and clear arm signals when giving your decisions. Your signals are important methods of communicating to everyone, who the free-kick or throw has been awarded to.

Give decisions with authority: e.g., when two opposing players challenge for a ball near the touchline, and it is debatable whose throw-in it should be when the ball goes out of play: blow your whistle hard - players will then look in your direction; (hopefully, this will discourage any scuffling for the ball) then signal in a positive and confident manner.

This works, because the truth of the matter is, there will probably be nobody present who will be absolutely sure - including yourself on occasions. But as long as you look certain of yourself, others will be convinced. And, remember - your decision is final and has to be accepted.

When indicating the direction of a free-kick or throw-in, hold your arm out nice and straight, and parallel to the ground. If you are giving an indirect free-kick, your arm should be pointing straight up, and brushing against an ear.

Good Communication - Good Self-Presentation

Take Responsibility - Give 100% Effort

Set yourself high standards with these things in mind, and you could go far in refereeing.

CHAPTER 8

Use Your Experience and Avoid Being Too Clever!

Life is full of ups and downs - sometimes we do the right things - and sometimes the wrong things.

As Alan Seville once wisely said to me:

"The only person who never makes a mistake, is the person who never does anything."

Experience, in all walks of life, is about making decisions; some right and some wrong.

This applies very much so to soccer refereeing. All referees make mistakes - we are only human after all. But the good referee is the referee that admits to the mistakes he makes, and learns from them. This is what makes the Referees Association meetings such useful occasions. There you can talk openly with other referees about your problems.

Listen to the advice offered to you - especially from the more experienced ones. Never be afraid that other referees will laugh at your mistakes, because they have almost certainly made the same ones; and, in all probability, some far worse than yours. Even the top referees make the occasional blunder, so remember when you do slip up, you are in good company

Let us look now at a good example of this; an incident that taught Alan Seville to always...

Avoid Being too Clever

A friend of Alan's once offered him a piece of philosophy: "These players that kick the ball away in temper when they've been penalised should be made to bring it back themselves."

Alan thought this was an idea that might be worth trying. He was at the time very young, and had ony recently started refereeing in open-age football.

He very soon had the opportunity to test his friend's 'inspirational suggestion.' In fact, it was during his next game.

One of the players handled the ball: Alan duly blew for the offence and the player bad-temperedly walloped the ball away, many a mile. The ball was returned, by another player, to the spot where Alan was cautioning the offending player.

When he had finished his writing, Alan picked up the ball and booted it away - with interest.

"There you are," said our hero, slightly triumphantly. "You kicked it away, so now you can go and fetch it yourself!"

The player stood, hands on hips, looking thoughtfully down at the future "smallest man in black in the business." I imagine he was taking into consideration the fact that he had already been booked for the offence, and was now safe in that respect, before saying: "No, ref, you kicked it away - so you can fetch it yourself!"

Poor old Alan. There was nothing he could do about it. Nowhere in the rules of football is there anything that says a referee can make a player retrieve a ball.

So Alan learned from this that the only punishments a referee can dish out to an erring footballer are those present in the laws - never make up your own rules.

Use Your Experience and Avoid Being Too Clever!

When I was attending my Referee's Course, one of the things we were told was to always stand on the goal-line when a corner-kick was being taken. No doubt you will have seen Football League referees positioned well off the goal-line during professional games. The reason for this is that they have official, and therefore impartial, linesmen to assist them. They will normally be instructed by the referee to stand on the goal-line and act as goal judges during the taking of a corner-kick.

But here we are dealing with club linesmen and, as I indicated previously, you should give them as little responsibility as possible and take responsibility yourself.

CHAPTER 9

Take Responsibility

I have highlighted one of Mr Seville's miscalculations for the purpose of demonstration, so I think it is only fair to use a couple of my own for the same reason.

The first is with reference to the positioning at corner-kicks:

It was a Cup semi-final, in which one of the teams competing was entirely made up of Greek players.

They were soon 2-0 up and well on top, looking certain winners. They forced a corner on their left-wing. I decided to take up a position, not on the goal-line as I had always done previously, but just inside the penalty-area.

(The only reason I can give for this is that I thought I might gain a better view of any pushing and shoving that could occur. The truth of the matter is, in the dozen or so games I had already refereed, there had not been one 'was it over the line or wasn't it?' situation. But things have a nasty way of happening when you are not prepared for them.)

The corner-kick was taken. Attacking and defending heads strove to connect with the ball. An attacking head won and a goal looked certain till the goalkeeper launched himself across goal, knocking the ball away. There was a tremendous scramble then: feet were flying and the ball ricocheted crazily, like the steel one in a pinball-machine.

Then a player got a clear shot on goal: I saw the goalkeeper fling himself backwards, this time scooping the ball out from behind him. The Greek

Soccer Refereeing - Whistling for Fun

players close by all jumped up in the air in celebration; but though it looked to me to be possibly over the line, from my position I could not be certain. I looked across at the defending team's linesman for help - he was perfectly placed to judge - but he simply shrugged his shoulders; I was on my own.

I shouted to the players to 'play on' which most of them did. But one fellow just followed me all over the pitch, ranting and raving. I had no idea what it was he was saying, because he was doing so in his own language - in fact, you might say it was all Greek to me.

After that, the Greeks' Latin temperament got the better of them; I cautioned four of their players, and the team seemed to go to pieces.

The other side got two quick goals to level the score, and extra-time had to be played, the Greeks losing 3-2 in that period.

I felt upset that because of my poor positioning, the Greeks had been denied a possible winning 3-0 lead. So learn from my mistake - it was a basic error of judgement - and there is no need for you to commit the same error:

Always stand on the goal-line at corner-kicks when club-linesmen are being used.

My final example of what not to do, will illustrate why it is extremely important that you watch play at all times.

CHAPTER 10

Watch Play At All Times

To do what the above heading says may seem all too obvious to you, and you probably think that you would not dream of doing otherwise. But I will now prove just how easy it is to fall into the trap of 'doing otherwise.'

The game in which the 'otherwise' occurred was being played on a very muddy pitch. A defender thumped the ball out of defence and towards the opposition penalty-area. One of his team-mates was in pursuit of it, having got clear of the defence. I was not far behind him, trying to keep up with play.

The goalkeeper had seen the danger and came galloping off his line, just managing to claim the ball before the forward reached it.

So that was the picture: the goalie standing with his arms wrapped protectively around the ball; the opposing forward standing in front of him. Seeing this, I began running backwards towards the halfway-line, in anticipation of the goalkeeper's clearance. (Here, I would just like to say that running backwards should be an essential ingredient of your fitness training. There are occasions during a game when you want to change your position on the pitch without taking your eyes off the action. Back-pedalling enables you to do this.)

So there I was, back-pedalling for all I was worth, with a good view of the situation and everything under control. Then, just as I was arriving at my desired spot on the pitch, I heard a groan behind me. I took a quick look - there on the ground sat a player holding his knee, obviously in

Soccer Refereeing - Whistling for Fun

pain. I checked back and saw that the goalkeeper and forward had not moved... Well - what could go wrong? I turned back to the injured player, but now took the time to ask if he required attention.

Three seconds I averted my eyes from the 'keeper and the forward - but a lot can happen in three seconds of a football match... suddenly there were cries of "Penalty, referee", ringing in my ears.

I quickly switched my attention back to where the ball was - but the scene had now changed dramatically: the forward was sprawled in the mud, while the 'keeper was in the process of climbing to his feet, the ball still in his grasp.

"It's a penalty, ref'", the shouts continued insistently.

To say I was in a state of confusion would be the understatement of the millennium. The 'keeper was staring in my direction, still holding on tightly to the ball. The look on his face could have meant anything; shock - expectation - anxiety - GUILT.

But when I had recovered sufficiently from my own befuddled state to yell, "Play on. I didn't see it!" I saw there a definite expression of - RELIEF.

I knew then I had missed something important. I asked one of the 'keeper's team-mates what had happened, as I ran alongside him.

He explained, "Our 'keeper tried to bounce the ball and it stuck in the mud - their bloke knocked it past him, and was just about to stick it in the net, when our 'keeper pulled him down. Should have been a penalty, ref."

I had dropped a 'clanger' of the highest magnitude.

The game finished in a 1-1 draw.

When I had changed, I went into the changing-room of the team that should have been awarded the penalty. The players and their manager

Watch Play At All Times

were discussing the game. I explained about the injured player, then apologised for having failed to see the penalty incident. "All I can say is that I will never make that mistake again", I said. The attitude of the manager and his players was excellent. The manager said he knew it was a genuine mistake and urged me not to worry about it.

It happens that I had refereed this team several times before, the manager always being appreciative of my efforts. The fact is, we had struck up a good relationship.

I think his reaction to my error shows the profit there is to be gained from getting on with people as best as you can: the evidence is there, too, that football people have respect for the referee who can admit to being wrong.

I thought it might be a fitting way to finish by touching on the method of referee promotion. The system used is called the Pyramid system.

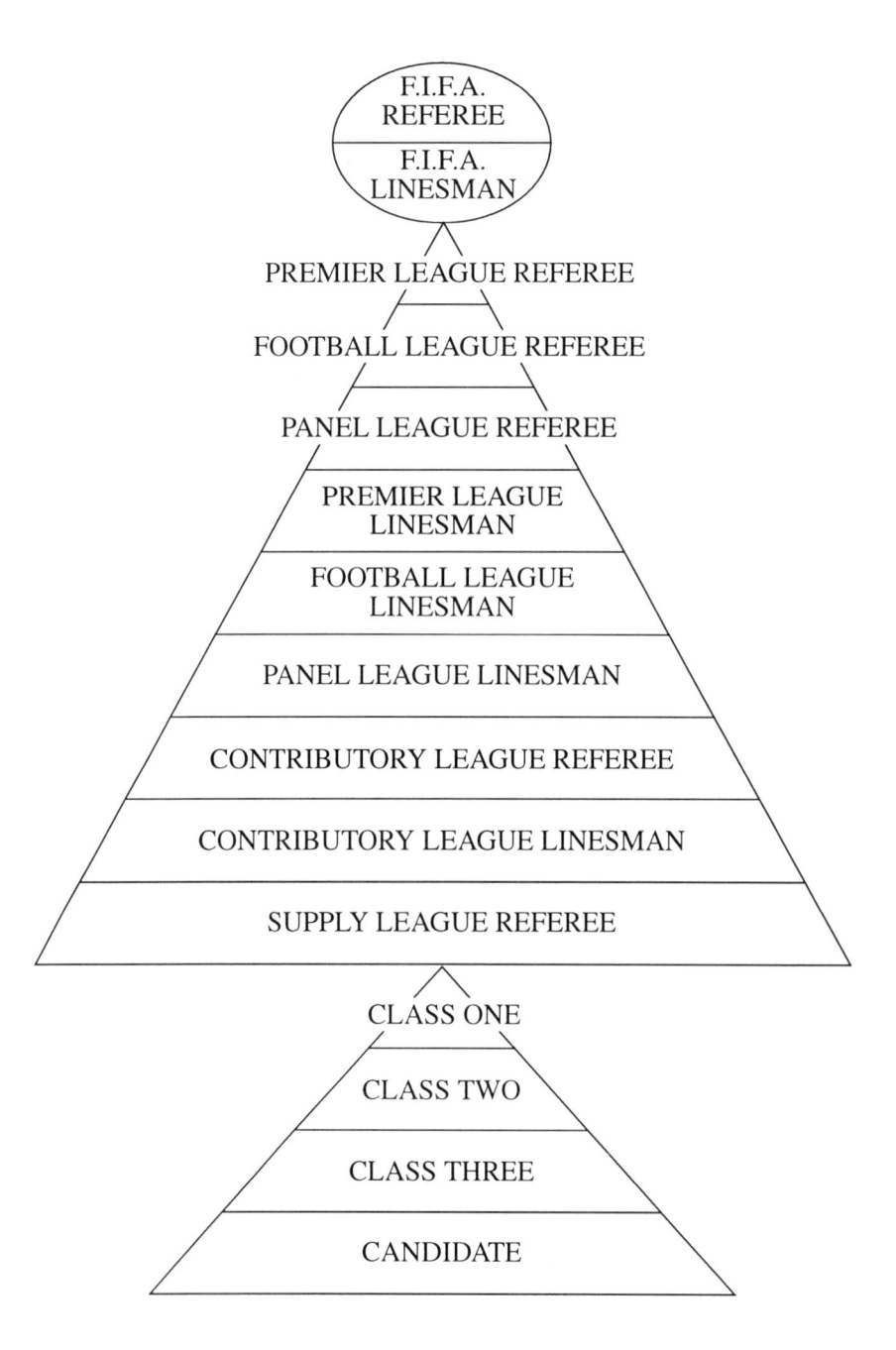

```
         _____
        /   F.I.F.A. \
       (   REFEREE    )
        \   F.I.F.A.  /
         \  LINESMAN /
          -----------
         /\
   PREMIER LEAGUE REFEREE
        /\
   FOOTBALL LEAGUE REFEREE
        /\
    PANEL LEAGUE REFEREE
       /            \
      / PREMIER LEAGUE \
     /    LINESMAN      \
    /--------------------\
   /   FOOTBALL LEAGUE    \
  /       LINESMAN         \
 /--------------------------\
/     PANEL LEAGUE LINESMAN  \
/------------------------------\
/    CONTRIBUTORY LEAGUE REFEREE \
/----------------------------------\
/    CONTRIBUTORY LEAGUE LINESMAN    \
/--------------------------------------\
/         SUPPLY LEAGUE REFEREE          \
/-----------------------------------------\
              CLASS ONE
              CLASS TWO
             CLASS THREE
              CANDIDATE
```

CHAPTER 11

The 'Pyramid' System

The diagram on page 42 shows exactly why the system is named thus: at the bottom of the pile there are the Candidates. These are simply the many people who embark on referee coaching courses all over the country.

Some will possibly not finish the course, and others may fail the examination at the end of it. The ones that complete it successfully will be registered as Class Three referees.

This sort of 'natural wastage' continues from Class Three, upwards to the very top - hence the 'Pyramid'.

From the hundreds of people who began as Candidates, there will be some with ambition to reach the 'dizzy heights': others will simply find their level; the standard of football at which they are perhaps comfortable.

As part of this book is intended as an introduction to refereeing for youngsters, I think it would be unwise and confusing to go into too much detail of the higher grades.

However, for the inquisitive, and perhaps more ambitious, ones amongst you, here is a brief chronicle.

Look at the diagram and you can see that once you have attained the Status of Class One, you become what is called a **'Supply League'** referee.

Soccer Refereeing - Whistling for Fun

Then you are introduced progressively into each of the leagues, first as a linesman. As such, you will be part of a team, partnered by another linesman, who will probably have a similar amount of experience to yourself. The third member of this team is, of course, the referee.

In this situation, the referee will always be a more experienced official than his linesmen. This makes the 'Pyramid' System the excellent learning process it is.

As referees progress upwards from junior football through semi-professional level, then into the Football League set-up, their methods of refereeing alter. Of course, the same set of rules must apply whatever standard one referees in; nevertheless there is a gradual but definite modification in refereeing style.

By watching and learning from the more experienced referee, this alteration in their approach is, by necessity, achieved by degrees through the 'Pyramid' System.

It used to be that the most likely age at which an official might join the list of linesmen on the Football League, was between 33-36; but it is true that some are now managing to do so in their 20's.

At the time of writing, the retirement age for Football League referees is 48 and for linesmen 44. However, these limits are, at this moment in time, being reduced; this means that younger referees will be promoted if their ability demands it.

So that is a quick look at how the system works; now, let us come back to earth and talk about what really is a 'Pyramid' System on its own: the journey from Class Three to Class One.

Generally speaking, promotion from Class Three to Class Two can be achieved in two to three seasons. Providing you have achieved a

The 'Pyramid' System

reasonable average mark in that time, promotion is more or less automatic.

From Two to One is rather different. There is a specified average mark that must be attained, then each referee is assessed by an Area Assessor. (This person is usually an experienced referee or ex-referee himself.)

There are four of these assessments made; the reports from these will then join the match marks you have attained through the season, at County headquarters. There they are scrutinized and your fate is decided.

That's it in a nutshell really; except to say that with dedication, a bit of luck and the wind in the right direction, it is possible to reach Class One in four years.

So, by the time you have reached the age of twenty, you could be well on your way up that pyramid.

But whatever happens, whatever level you reach, remember: WHISTLE FOR FUN.

**Jack Swain during his Grimsby Town
days before the war.**

CHAPTER 12

Jack Swain - the first of the few

When Jack Swain returned to Grimsby after serving in the army during the Second World War, he decided against returning to life as a professional footballer and entered the teaching profession. Having played for Grimsby Town in the First Division from 1936-1939, this career move enabled him to complete a unique first which few, if any, have achieved.

In 1946 sporting his army battledress appropriately dyed black, he became a referee in the local football league and, such was his progress that, within only 3 or 4 years, he became a linesman in the prestigious Midland League. At that time the Midland League enjoyed a status not far short of the current GM/Vauxhall Conference. As a consequence, referees appointed to the Midland League were frequently called upon as linesmen in the Football League. Thus in the early 1950's in an amazingly short period of time by current standards, Jack was placed on the League list and became the first ex-professional footballer to achieve such a distinction.

It is interesting to note that his success must have had a favourable influence on his fellow Grimsby referees because, in the 1957-58 season there were no fewer than three Grimsby-based referees on the League list - Jack, Arthur Sparling and Jack Topliss - this from a town with a population at the time of around 90,000.

CHAPTER 13

Personal Recollections

Finally, I thought that you might like to share in one of my personal refereeing memories - only the names have been changed to protect the innocent!

One evening I received a phone call from the secretary of a local Sunday League. "How would you like a tough game this weekend, Barry?" he asked.

"They're all tough", I replied. "Yes, but this could be very, very tough", he said. He then told me the name of the antagonists due to take part in the expected bloodbath. I was familiar with one of the sides - St. Sids. In one of their games, I had needed to perform what was tantamount to a whistling concerto. For the duration of that game my whistle had rarely been out of my mouth. And when I wasn't whistling, I was writing. I cautioned six of their players, for their various wrongdoings. It wasn't that they were a dirty side so much as a niggly, irritating team, who seemed more interested in stopping the other side from enjoying their game, than doing anything that resembled playing football. They employed blatant obstruction, shirt-pulling, sly trips, dissent by word and action, and kicking the ball away when penalised - all the offences that might have been designed by some form of Soccer anti-Christ to denigrate the character of the greatest sport there is.

The game will always remain in my memory as one that contained one of the most bizarre episodes I have experienced in football. During the first half I had occasion to caution a player by the name of Nelson. I made what turned out to be a vain and fruitless effort to lighten the atmosphere

Soccer Refereeing - Whistling for Fun

of the proceedings by injecting a little humour. "No relation of the late Lord Nelson I assume," I said, my pencil hovering above my little notebook, while I flashed him a smile that said, 'you see, I make jokes, so I am human after all.' He came back with the sourest of scowls and then stumped off back to the area of the pitch in which he 'operated', without grunting a word.

I blew the whistle for half-time a couple of minutes later. Mr. Nelson passed by me as he left the pitch, and treated me to a look which plainly did not say, 'I think you were absolutely right to book me Mr. Referee.'

I was standing alone in the centre-circle, thinking about all the other things I would rather be doing than reffing this particular game, when I heard the sound of footsteps behind me. It was the manager of St. Sids. He was a man with an extremely gloomy sort of face, and when he spoke I found that it was matched by his voice.

"Yo' ain't 'alf upset ma player referee," he said. His accent was thick Black Country, but without that lovely uppy downy lilt, peculiar to the accent of the industrial heart of England. "Yo' should be careful what yo' say t'peeple."

I had not the slightest idea what he was talking about, and just stared at him. I couldn't help thinking that his words were a little ironical, considering the fact that his team had just spent forty-five minutes upsetting me. Without waiting for me to speak, he carried on in the same un-Black Country-like monotone.

"Charlie Nelson. Yo've really upset 'im yo' 'ave. I can't get a word out of 'im."

I thought this must be some sort of Black Country wind-up - surely nobody could be that sensitive about their name. All the same, more out of curiosity than anything else, I found myself strolling over to where St. Sids were sucking alternately on their oranges and fags.

Personal Recollections

There was one player stood apart from the rest. Sure enough - it was Charlie. He was busy excavating mud from down his fingernails. He looked up as I approached him. Before I could speak, he did an about turn, presenting me with a back view of himself.

"Excuse me, er - Charlie," I said to his back. He walked forward a couple of paces. I followed him. "I'm sorry if I offended you in some way." He took two more paces - I followed. "I didn't mean anything by it. It was just a joke." Charlie then astonished me by walking away, then squeezing himself into a little ruck of four or five of his team mates, who were stood talking. He was acting like a petulant, Hollywood film star. He peered out at me from his apparent cocoon of safety. I gave up then. To be honest, it was a situation I didn't quite know how to handle. But it taught me to not assume that all footballers are blessed with a sense of humour. I have never since passed any comment about players' names, jokingly or otherwise.

Well that was St. Sids. Their forthcoming opponents, whom I shall call Redcard United, I knew only by reputation... Earlier in the season a referee had abandoned a game in which they were involved - he had been unable to control them. The week before that, the ref in charge of their game had had a trainer's bucket bounced off his head. I thought it sounded like quite a challenge...

On arrival at the ground, I informed the two managers that I was present. The atmosphere in both dressing-rooms was quiet and indicated no cause for anxiety on my part. In fact the first half an hour or so of the game, proved to be almost incident-free. The only suggestion of a problem was in the shape of a Redcard player whom I shall call Wally Windger. He stood around six-feet tall, and was in fact very skilful. He played as a forward and had the skill and speed to beat defenders at will. But he was also a moaner. Several times early in the game, whenever suffering from any suggestion of physical contact, he would simply stop playing and

Soccer Refereeing - Whistling for Fun

begin complaining that he should have a free kick. However on none of these occasions did I consider he had been fouled, and consequently allowed play to continue each time. I was not a popular ref with our Wal'.

A few minutes before half-time, the first hint of bother materialised. A Redcard player deliberately handled the ball, and I blew for the foul. He promptly kicked the ball away, whereupon I cautioned him for dissent. This was the only real disturbance of the first half. So at half-time, I was sending thank-you messages up to my good old guardian angel for his apparent presence. But if he was with me in that first half, I think he must have been called away on another assignment in the second. As I blew the whistle to restart the game, I hadn't long to wait for the fireworks to begin.

The chap who I had already booked was the first for the 'early bath.' He apparently wanted to find out what one of the opposing players would look like with just the one leg. His scything kick landed just above the poor bloke's knee, and the wonder was that nothing was broken. It could only be described as a deliberate assault. There wasn't any way the player could have reached the ball with his boot, so he simply kicked the nearest object he could reach. Minutes later, a St. Sids forward, sporting yellow 'punk' hair, was racing down the touchline in pursuit of the ball. A Redcard central defender galloped out from his territory, obviously intent on halting his opponent. To be fair, the slide-tackle that ensued was as legal as it was effective. The intervening foot played the ball first and the straw-haired forward a split-second later. With the weight of the tackle, the two of them finished up three or four yards off the pitch. Call me psychic if you like, but I arrived on the scene before the dust had settled, hopefully to prevent any trouble. But I wasn't quite quick enough, and when I reached them they were sat on their backsides, examining the texture of each other's hair - both grasping a healthy

Personal Recollections

handful, whilst delivering a punch or two with their free hands.

A couple of St. Sids players began trying to prise their pal away from this scalp-stretching contest, but the Redcard players were notable by their absence. It was a Mexican stand off. Neither seemed prepared to relinquish his hold on the other's thatch. So yours truly, (in breach of all the advice given about not touching players) shoved my fingers up the tackler's nostrils and exerted upward pressure. (In my own defence, I swear I think we would all still have been there now, had I not performed this damp and distasteful action.) The recipient of my nasal attack loosed his hold immediately, pivoting around on his bum to see who was responsible for this cowardly attack on his hooter. But, though old and decrepit, I was still lightish on my feet and had stepped back smartly after extricating my fingers. In different circumstances, I might have laughed at the dumbfounded look on the player's face, but I had to bury the smile that threatened, under an expression of unforgiving authority.

After listening unsympathetically to the pleas for forgiveness from the Redcard player, I expelled the pair from the pitch. When he saw that his pleading had gone in one ear and out the other, he reverted to type and demonstrated his knowledge of foul and abusive language.

Four more Redcard players were cautioned before the fourth sending off, ten minutes from the final whistle. It was my friend Wally Windger who had to go this time. The ball had been floated down the middle towards the St. Sids goal, where W.W. was lurking. But the harshness of life being what it is, he was flagged offside. I blew my whistle which halted W.W. in his tracks. He threw me a murderous look. Meanwhile, the St. Sids 'keeper had picked the ball up and advanced to where W.W. stood, still looking at me with something less than affection. As the goalie went to place the ball on the floor for the free-kick, Windger went suddenly berserk. He wildly kicked out at the ball which was still in the goalkeeper's hands. The ball flew up in the air and the 'keeper dropped to his

Soccer Refereeing - Whistling for Fun

knees, holding his left arm in agony. I was standing only ten yards or so away, and I have to admit that I had to remind myself that I was a referee. I was so angry with what I had witnessed, it took enormous self-control on my part not to give him a taste of his own medicine. Instead, I contented myself with bawling down his ear as loudly as I could, that I should like him to leave the field of play please… "Gerroff!" I yelled, whilst pointing in the direction of the dressing-rooms. I think I must have put the wind up him a little, for he suddenly marched quickly away from me. Then from about thirty yards distance, he began yelling obscenities at me in a most hysterical manner. "You're too old to be a referee anyway," is about the only printable bit of speech in the torrent of abuse he aimed at me.

It was with a certain amount of relief that I blew up for full-time, a few minutes later. But the high jinks didn't end there. The next fifteen minutes were to prove quite eventful.

As I made my way off the pitch, I was thinking quickly back through the game. The old enemy, self-doubt, presented itself in my mind. Was I 'too old to be a referee?' At the time I was forty-two, and certainly had never thought of myself as too old previously to this moment. Happily, I was rescued from my negative frame of mind, by one of the forty or so spectators who had been watching the match.

"Well done, ref. You had a great game." He was probably in his twenties, and judging by his firm handshake, his words were sincere. "Well done," he repeated, than ran off to rejoin his mates (perhaps not wanting to be seen fraternising with a referee). Then my old friend the St. Sids manager confronted me. "Yo'll 'ave to mek a report out ref," he said, in soporific tone. "Ma player's been attacked in the dressing-room by that bloody nutter yo' sent off with 'im."

"Attacked?" I said, beginning to think I was still in bed, and all of this was a result of the cheese and pickle sandwich I had eaten the night

Personal Recollections

before.

"Are. 'it 'im on the 'ead with his boot 'e did." Just then the lad with the yellow hair joined us. "Eeyar, look at the stud marks on 'is forrid," said his manager, his voice almost rising with excitement.

And indeed there they were - slap bang in the middle of his 'forrid'. But they were more dents than marks. I was beginning to wonder what these people were putting in the half-time cuppa these days.

I told him that because I had not seen what had occurred, I could only report it as heresay, but that it would certainly be in my report.

I continued then on my way to the dressing-room. It was then I learned another valuable lesson - after a game where teams such as Redcard have performed in such a manner, always allow the players to leave the scene of battle before yourself... I suppose I was lucky the thrower had a poor aim - the football hurled from behind me, missed my head by a good two feet. I looked over my shoulder and glared as menacingly as I could. There were players from both teams but I had a shrewd idea from which camp the missile had been launched. The second football nicked my ear (they say that practice makes perfect). This time I spun around to face them, which resulted in every one of them halting in their tracks.

"If that happens again there's going to be trouble," I shouted through gritted teeth. At this point I must ask you, reader, not to put me up on a pedestal as some sort of hero. In all honesty I knew I was on fairly safe ground in making this statement - I had noticed earlier that Redcard were in possession of only two footballs.

At last I reached the sanctuary of the referee's dressing-room. I had just finished taking my boots off, when in walked the Redcard manager. He presented me with the team sheet and my match expenses. As he did this, his eyes fired daggers at me.

Soccer Refereeing - Whistling for Fun

"Thank you," I said, more politely than he deserved. He was everything I disliked in the world of soccer. All through the second half of the game, he had been urging his players to be physically intimidating. "Chop him down! Don't let him get past you," appeared to be one of his favourite war-cries.

He continued to glare at me as I handed him back the paperwork. "You ruined that ******* game," he said, his face held only a couple of inches from my own, while he poked me in the chest with a provoking finger.

"I don't think so," I replied without moving away. "You can take all the credit for that yourself. I can see now where the players get their attitude problems from." Unbelievably, he thrust his face even closer. "What are you going to do about it then?" he said. Again I restrained myself, then employed the one legal weapon at my disposal. "Well, before you leave this dressing-room, I'll have your name please." The book and pencil were in my hand before he could blink.

"Don't know what you want my name for," he said, easing away from me now, the aggression in his voice having receded. "I'm nothing to do with the club."

This statement was made despite my having seen him in the dressing-room before the match, giving the players their kit, as well as dishing out the oranges at half-time. And then there was the small matter of me warning him about his inflammatory remarks during the game, to which he had replied: "I can say what I like. I'm the manager."

As I expected, he refused to give his name. But that was easy to turn up. I simply asked his opposite number, who was only too pleased to oblige: "They'm a right bloody family ay they ref?" he droned. I asked him what he meant. "Well two of they players yo' sent off was 'is sons wo' they?" Enough said, I think.

I had a lot of writing to do that evening. As well as making out the

Personal Recollections

necessary report forms, I wrote two letters - one to the relevant League Secretary, and the other to the Birmingham County F.A. I asked that strong action be taken against Redcard. In my letter to the League Secretary, I made it plain that if Redcard were still operating in the League in the following season then I certainly would not be. The upshot of this was, a few weeks later, I received a letter from the League Secretary inviting me to an extraordinary meeting at League headquarters. In the letter he congratulated me on my strong handling of the game, and informed me that the St. Sids player who had been attacked, was bringing legal action against his assailant. This pleased me no end. I found it very gratifying to think that justice might well be seen to be done, and that this awful team would get their come uppance.

The hall was tightly packed for the meeting, which had been called purely to give people associated with the league, a chance to vote whether or not Redcard should remain within that league. The result was a massive majority to boot them out. Obviously they had upset quite a few people on their way, with their anti-social antics.

I saw the League Secretary after the meeting closed, and asked him why Redcard had been allowed to get away with things for so long. He said, "You're the first referee to put pen to paper, and I'd like to thank you for that." We shook hands, and I went away wondering how any referee could put up with the sort of thing I had witnessed in that match without doing anything about it. But I also felt disappointed that a league should depend on one person to bring about some sort of justice. Surely a club's disciplinary record should determine whether or not it has a place in any football competition.

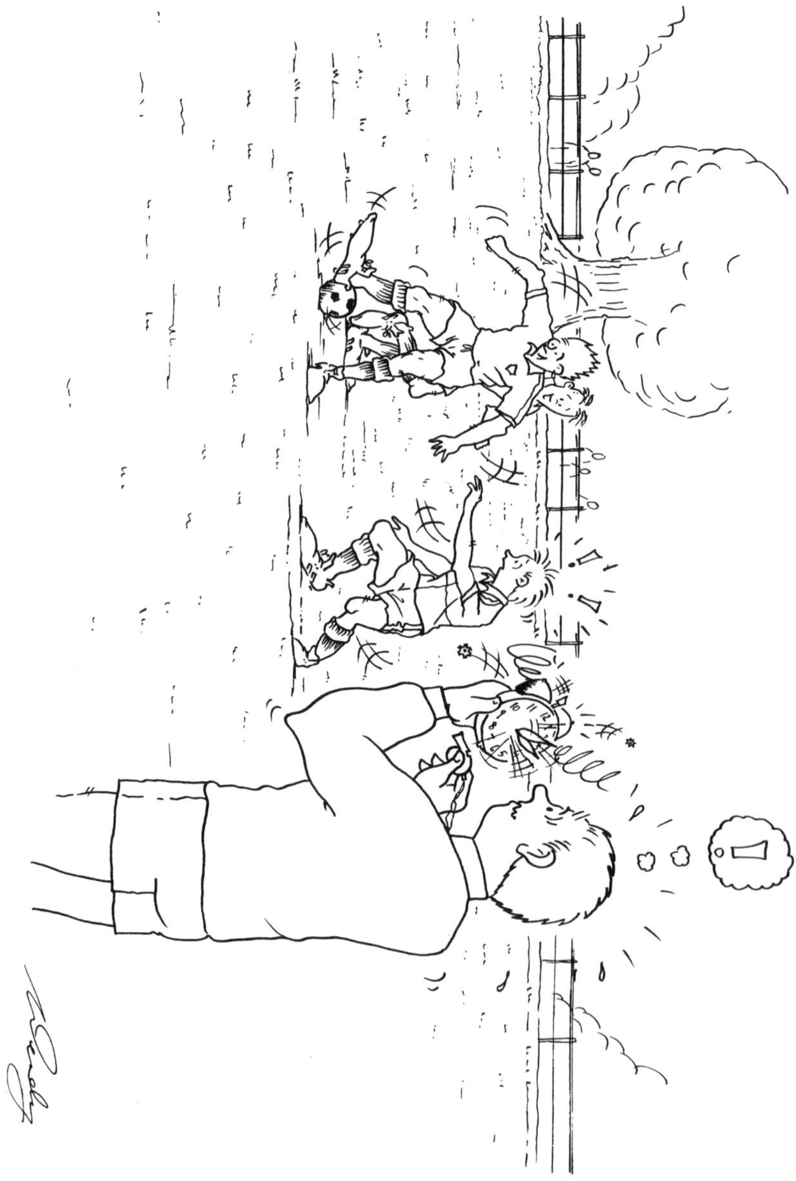

CHAPTER 14

Refereeing Nightmares
of a retired referee

My very first game as a referee was one which I will never forget. Having played for the previous two seasons for a local team, I was amazed to find myself allocated as the match referee for their first game of the new season. To make matters worse, it was my old team's home tie and I consequently found myself sitting in my old club's dressing room - in my usual place.

The first hint of a problem arose when, having exchanged pleasantries with my old team-mates, the club manager threw me a set of the club's strip and told me I was playing at left-back. When I told him I was actually the referee, he was gobsmacked and tore off home to get his boots - to play instead of me!

The game itself went fine - no trouble from either side - and with the scoreline 2-1 to my old club, I blew for the end of the game. As I went back to the changing room, the manager of the other team approached me with a strange look on his face.

"Do you realise that you have only played 30 minutes in the second-half?" he asked. I didn't, but when I looked at my watch, it suddenly advanced another ten minutes - a sort of quantum leap.

"Right, everyone back," I shouted as, borrowing the manager's watch, I took them back for another 15 minutes. Thank goodness neither side came close to scoring during this 'extra time' and I learned one of the first lessons of refereeing - carry two watches!

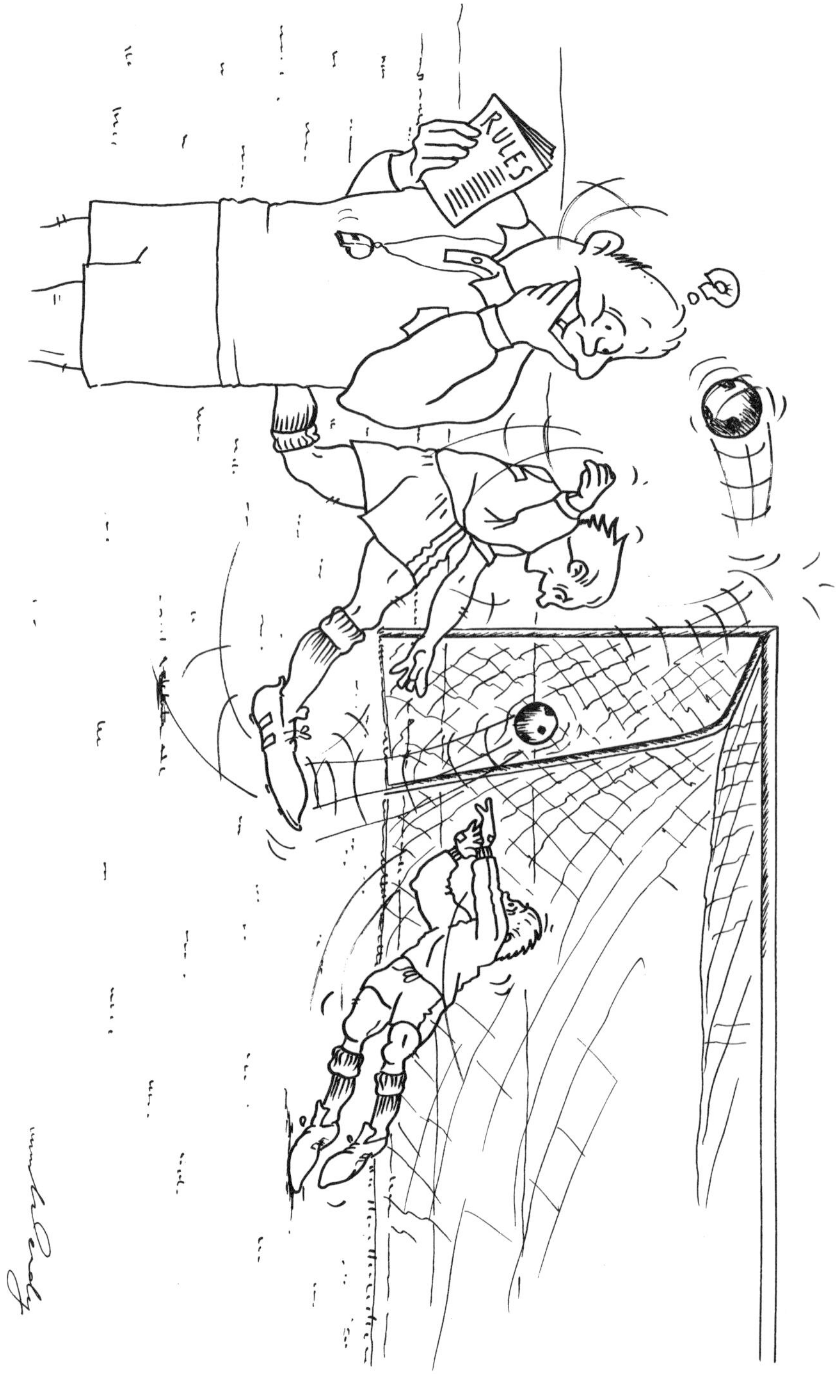
RULES

Refereeing Nightmares

Have you ever played on a local authority football pitch which has only about ten feet between it's goal-line and that of the adjoining pitch? I have, or rather I have refereed on such a pitch and it certainly caused me a problem.

It was a close-fought game between two of the less-able local sides and the attacking team had just won a corner on their left side. As the corner was taken, the match ball from the game on the adjacent pitch soared over our goalmouth and, to my dismay, struck the ball being centred from the corner kick. The fact that one of the balls bounced out into touch, whilst the other was volleyed into the roof of the net caused yet another problem. The attacking team claimed the goal, the defending team protested and both teams suggested I should examine the ball from the back of the net to see if it was the one from our game.

I didn't bother, but told them to find the right ball and retake the corner again as the intrusion of the other ball was 'interference with play.'

After the game, both managers approached me to discuss the decision and were of the opinion that, according to the rules, there should have been a bounce-up at the point of impact. My reply was quite simple - "Probably, but how could we have done that 15 feet above the ground!"

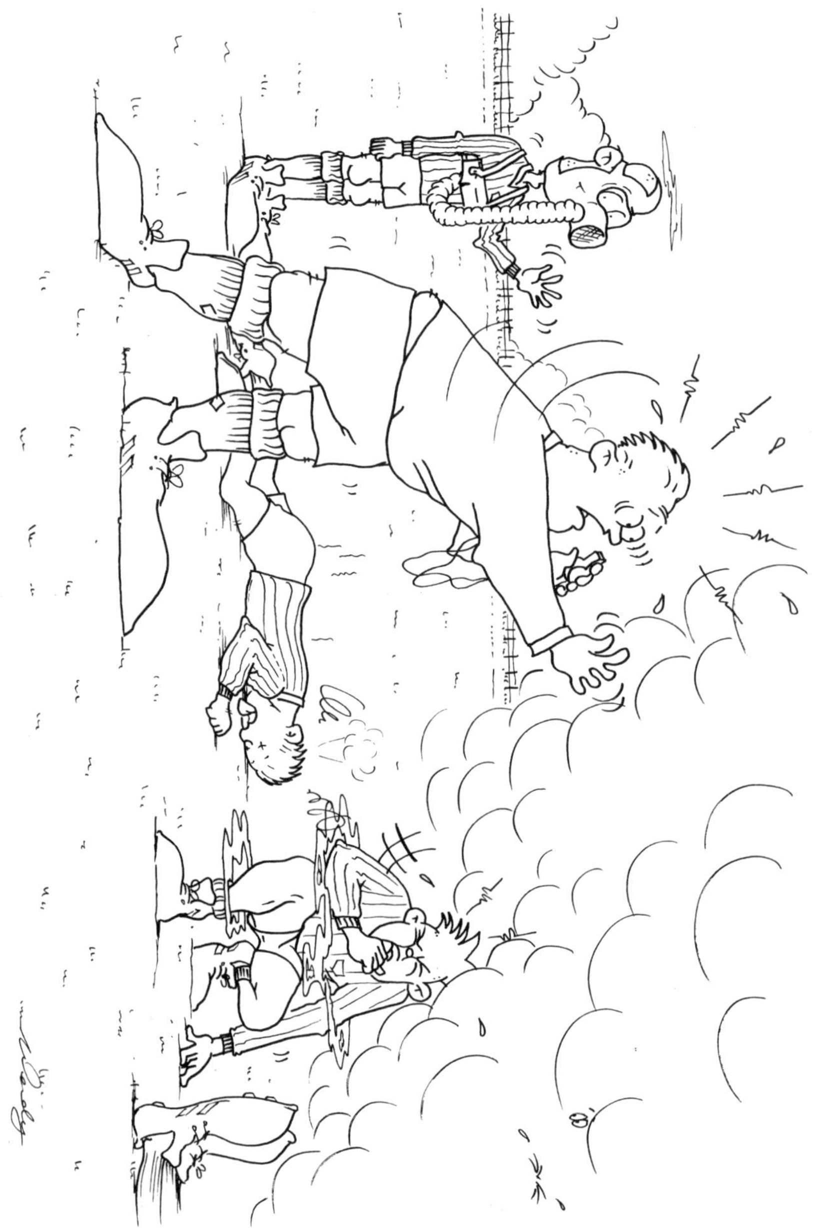

Refereeing Nightmares

It was a beautiful sunny Sunday morning - perfect for football, crisp and clear. The game which I was refereeing was a lower-league meeting between two young teams from neighbouring villages, not a needle match but keenly contested.

Midway through the second-half with the scoreline tied on 2-2, a gardener from the adjacent village allotments decided it was time to light a bonfire to dispose of his rubbish. Unfortunately, a light breeze was blowing across our pitch directly from the allotments and, as the fire took hold, clouds of billowing brown smoke drifted across the halfway line.

It was no more than a nuisance at first and, despite stinging eyes and occasional coughs, we continued the game without problems. Then it happened - the old man piled a load of wet grass onto his bonfire and the smoke went into 'peasoup mode!' A cloud of choking smoke rolled across the pitch and the ball disappeared from view. Just as I raised my whistle to stop play, a cheer came up from the murk and the attackers emerged from the smoke celebrating a goal.

I disallowed the goal without hesitation and despite a few grumbles, the attackers went along with the decision - after all the poor old goalie had no chance when the shot whistled into the net from a cloud of smoke!

Strange Refereeing Occurrences

In a 1975 Chile versus Uruguay international in Santiago, Chilian referee, Sergio Vasquez sent off a total of 19 players after a free-for-all fight, 10 of whom were from the home side. A few days later, the unfortunate referee was suspended and fined by the Chilean Referees' Association for losing control of the match.

Another South American referee, Hector Rodriguez of Uruguay, marked his first international game in 1977 by sending off six players from the Ecuadorian team in a game against Uruguay in Montevideo. The match was eventually abandoned with the score at 1-1.

Henning Erikstrup, the referee in charge of a match in between Noerager and Ebeltoft in Denmark in 1960, received protests from Ebeltoft players after blowing for time. Noerager were winning 4-3 when Mr. Erikstrup decided to blow his whistle to signal the end of the match. However, as he was about to blow, his false teeth fell out and whilst he was retrieving them Ebeltoft equalised. Mr. Erikstrup put his teeth back in, ruled out the goal and blew for time, waving aside Ebeltoft protests.